Larry Gavin | *A Fragile Shelter*

LARRY GAVIN

A Fragile Shelter

NEW AND SELECTED POEMS

Red Dragonfly Press

Copyright © 2019 by Larry Gavin
All rights reserved

ISBN 978-1-945063-29-9 paper

Library of Congress Control Number: 2019948140

These poems were performed, printed, reproduced or broadcast in the following places. The author thanks them.

Southwest Minnesota State University, KAXE radio, Grand Rapids, Minnesota, *The Minnesota Conservation Volunteer*, *Your Daily Poem*, The Paradise Center for the Arts, Faribault, MN Southcentral CommunityCollege, Sakata reading series, Mallard Island, Oberholtzer Foundation, *Trout Unlimited Minnesota*, The Bristol Bay Lodge, Alaska, Bob White artist series, The Laureate Reading Series: Northfield and Winona, Sweet Reads Bookstore and Artworks Festival, Austin, Minnesota, Blue Parlor Reading Series, Ripton Vermont, and St. John's University Sante Fe New Mexico, *Gray's Sporting Journal*, Crossings at Carnegie, Zumbrota Minnesota, The Rural American Writing Center, Plainview, Minnesota, The Anderson Center, Red Wing, Minnesota, Northern State University Aberdeen, South Dakota, *Poetic Strokes*, SELCO Library System, *The Minnesota English Journal*, *Pemmican*, Majors and Quinn bookstore. Looseleaf poetry series, Minneapolis.

A special thanks to Scott King for his hard work and great kindness.

Designed and typeset by Scott King at Red Dragonfly Press
   using Warnock Pro digital type

Published by Red Dragonfly Press
   P. O. Box 98
   Northfield, MN 55057

For more information and additional titles visit our website
   www.reddragonflypress.org

Contents

NECESSITIES (2003)

A Firefly Speaks   11
Northern Pike   13
Letter to a Friend   14
November   15
An Empty Shotgun Shell   16
An Old Dog Dreams   17
Falling Star: Winter   19
Ice Fishing At Winter Solstice   20
Cleaning Fish: December   21
Necessities   22
The Recluse at Ma's Café   23

LEAST RESISTANCE (2007)

Reminders   27
Sidewalk Sweeper: Mann's Chinese Theater   28
Throwing Shot Put   29
Photo Left on the Copy Machine   30
Police Report: A Found Poem   32
Irezumi   33
Passport Photograph   34
Telling the Bees   35
New Pens and a School Project at the Lower Sioux Agency   37
After Reading Octavio Paz I go Fish Walleyes in the Minnesota
    River   38
Conversation with a Girl Sculpting a Fist: Faribault Area
    Learning Center   40
Priming the Pump   41
I Close The Door   43
In Shadows   44
Maple and Fir   45
The Water Witch   46

After Reading Tu Fu I Go Off To Catch Rough Fish In the
    Cannon River 48
After Drinking with Friends I Write a Poem While Walking
    Home 49
October: Kewauni River 50
A Magician Daydreams 51
The Magician's Assistant 53
In Praise of Frogs 55
Waiting for all the Rest 57

Stone & Sky (2011)

On the Border 61
Reminder: Friday Night 62
Poem with a Line from Tom McGrath 63
Mouse 64
Firewood 65
Where the Bones 67
Two in Love 68
Gratitude 69
Writing with a New Pen, I Recall The Old Chinese Poets 70
Tired of What Is Beautiful 72
On Endings 73
What September Means 74
Stone and Sky 75

The Initiation of Praise (2014)

My Reader 79
The Table 80
Carp 81
Ground Nesting 82
Jubilee 83
Before Stepping 84
Digging Post Holes 85

Sweat Lodge: Morton, Minnesota 86
My Blood 87
The Stroke 88
Just Outside Aberdeen, South Dakota 89
Still 90
The Lie 91
Simulacrum 92
Ambition 93
Smelt Run 94
In Praise of Black Crappies 95
Walking Back to the Car: Kickapoo River 96
Let's Believe 97
Fereydoun Faryad in Northfield 98
On My Decision to Stop Writing Poetry 99
Imagine It 100
Misrepresented as Meaning: November 101
South Dakota 102
First Snow 103
Hailstones 104
After the Town Hall Forum 105

A Fragile Shelter (New Poems: 2017-2019)

A Hundred Fires 109
Rounding Out 110
On Your Fence Surviving a Late May Storm 111
End of Summer Love Poem 112
Ashes 114
What the Carp Taught Me 115
The Public Hearing 116
November Snow 117
Whitman Asleep 118
Poem for a Girl Reading the Odyssey at a Rest Area on Interstate 90 Near Fairmont, Minnesota 119
A Bear 120
After Illness 122

Plum Orchard   123
The Creel   124
Williston, North Dakota   125
Buffalo Gap National Grasslands   127
Addressing the Stones   128
Gideon's Marsh: November   129
To It All   130
At Dusk   131
At the Saw   132
The Hog   133
A Next Night   134
Moored   135
Monarch   136
Mending   137
Balance   138
After Death   139
A Picture Frame   140
Mallard Island: A Triptych   141
Pastoral   143
Cambrian Blackbirds   144
Daily Creek   145
School Begins   146
Wardrobe   147
Christmas Morning South of Faribault, MN   148
Deer at Six a.m.   149
Half the Table   150
No Leaving   151
Driving from Willow to Bee Creek   152
Brick Tender   153

About the Author

Necessities

(2003)

A Firefly Speaks

They were in love
I could see that
even in the dark.
It was his eyes
that gave it away,
their concentration
on her
words. The way she
insisted darkness
wasn't necessary
just desirable.
It was the word
desirable
obeying some order
I could only
guess at.
Obey.
Their embrace
was touching;
she touched his face.
They were like stars
fallen, cooling,
then heating up again.
I passed
obeying
air currents that just barely
pass through
the broken willow.
Their love
rubbed off on me.
I sing it in light
to darkness
building like
their love will build.

I know it.
I just know it.
It is happening now,
in the dark,
alone,
both of them.

Northern Pike

In the ripe green circle, of a white water lily's
shadow, down through the halo of surrounding
sunlight, spiked and wavering with refraction, forming
white blossoms from another world — magnificent
at the unspoken edge of curled pond weed and coon tail,
that create their own aquatic message of light
and shadow — edges left to be reassembled years from now
by some other, you, pike, are steady as a rooted thing
uniting worlds. No matter that you are seven inches long.
The angry is fused with the unpredictable
in your heart to become a story of consumption
gone wild: never satisfied. And that, dear pike,
is where our stories intersect. I am water and a handful
of less elegant elements when that water is removed:
carbon, calcium, and who knows what else? But the heart
beneath these elements, for now, is fine,
unsatisfied, and light. So let us sing together
of this world we share: of black nosed dace,
and perch, of bluegills and tadpoles and the space
between shadows from overhead, that protect
us both from too much light and what it sheds on sight.
Let's sing of cabbage weed and milfoil, of Richard's pond weed
and flat lily, of cattail, bulrush and sedge, and light
that makes this world our world. That sends us hints
that build from day to day, that are not satisfied by life
alone. The knowledge I am man not fish.
The tempered satisfaction we take in being still.

Letter to a Friend

Tonight we let the tomato
plants freeze
in the garden:
this a kind of letting go.
We let go, too,
of insects that buzz
around the porch light
and dew turned overnight
to frost
as surely as rain, one day,
will give way
to snow, slowly building.
And this morning Patty noticed teal
flocking up on Tim's slough.
She picked apples and turned them into pie,
so we share autumn and summer together
at the kitchen table.
We share the earlier evenings too
with all the wonder
the six o'clock news allows.
We try to remember one piece of good
advice we've ever received,
but tonight everything fits tight
in the toes
like mail order boots.
The hunter's moon hums
in the sky,
and the harvest goes on around us.
The dog circles three times
before lying down
which means a stranger will call.
We all wait in the dark,
think our own thoughts,
and hope for the best.

November

Bluebills pile up
on Tim's slough,
and the weatherman
more lost than normal
says : rain, sunshine, snow.
But we know, the dog and I,
that city weather does not apply here
in cattails, under a darkening sky.
We know, too,
these ducks have flown so far
ahead of this wind
they feel the own it
and by association
own the open water,
a kind of unmanageable daughter,
needing their attention
so they land
ending the way they began.

Behind them snow starts,
delicately at first,
a portent,
a sign,
a drifting, lacey reminder
that supper is cooking,
and that these days
darkness
always arrives
faster than light.

An Empty Shotgun Shell

Look into my center
and see light.
Laying here beside the crumbling fieldstone
corner post that marks Anderson land
in this county.
The dog, released, sniffs autumn
under blue sky
all bright eyes and movement fresh,
almost like starting over.
A milkweed bursts with late October,
and a pheasant cackles
from cattails
standing clean in sunlight.
A shotgun shell
red and brass
and tilted northwest
in dying grass.
A drop of dew
beaded near its base
reflects sun
perfect and distant
like permission to trespass.

An Old Dog Dreams

I know in your sleep,
old dog, you are not
an old dog,
but a creature outside of time.
Propelled by scent through a dream
unfolding like a flower in your
sleeping brain.
Scent melds taste to image
making all
an old dog needs to live,
the memory of scent, I mean.
In these final years
you seem to take nourishment
from air-made images
of pheasant, partridge, rabbit
grouse and autumn.
Smell charged with some strange
electricity as it signals
sleeping legs to run
in unrested slumber on the couch.
You chase pheasants across
the endless prairie at sunset don't you?
But now sunset made perfect.
You never fail to solve
the riddle of aroma
building to a powerful perfume at flush
brilliant as sunlight on cattails
in November.
I like to hope my smell
is there with you
I'd love to be timeless too
and stupid
as I was back then.
Until you, old dog,

taught me wisdom.
Wise to the ways of dogs
at least. The kind of wisdom
that arrives like a good dream
from who knows where
like fragrance, old age, and flight.

Falling Star: Winter

This Star
shaken from the sky
tumbles toward earth.
Erasing itself brilliantly
as it races itself
toward the horizon.
Like a tear
erases itself racing
down a cheek
toward despair
or a snowflake
erases itself
on a tongue
held out to heaven
sacramental and soundless.
But the eye suggests more
than memory
more than the unintentional
flight
from sky to earth
then out
perfect as starting over.
A heart looks to find
its place vacant
having just fallen here
joining us.

Ice Fishing At Winter Solstice

Sometimes I imagine
the darkness of late afternoon
exists to remind me of how surely
all light will disappear. There is no hesitation
as the sun, in heavy clouds, declines
behind hills, just as suddenly,
all thoughts of day vanish, too.
The cold rises with Venus, an evening
star this time of year.
The world becomes a circus of circles:
stars, the float, this hole
I stare into. I stare
as if a whole world depends on me
being here, and staring through a hole
in ice. Answering the old riddle
about what grows bigger the more
is taken away. I could count
my losses as losses, but tonight
the world begins its graceful slide
toward spring. Winter seems to pause
a moment; gathering itself suspended
in night, like bait suspended
by the float above the bottom,
like ice suspended above the density
of water air above ice and so on
into the infinite vacuum of space.
The float tugged beneath the surface
threatens to pull me down, too.
Instead, I draw the line tight
and set the hook.
I might as well be reeling in stars
reflected through dark water
to just within reach, becoming a fish
that can't live in air. My cold hands fold
around him as if in prayer.

Cleaning Fish: December

We gather
after dark
in the bare glow
of the basement light bulb
as if in church.
Believers together.
I slit the belly
and thumb out
the visceral parts
purple, red, pink,
internal colors we
all share.
The flesh,
nearly transparent,
slipped from skin
by the flexed blade
of a knife.
Leading to these small thoughts
of a soul set loose
in the world
then consumed
around the kitchen table.
My elbows
touching the elbows
of the ones I love.
Our real presence
in the world:
our appetite
for this life.

Necessities

These maple shade the back yard all summer
and erupt in orange and gold through
fall. Their dark roots draw me down
to earth each morning as I walk
touching them on bare ground
to conjure the coming day. In spring,
we tap them when the time is right
and gather as a family to watch
the first amber drops drip to the bottom
of the tin bucket, sounding to us like life.
We boil sap to reduce it by
three-quarters becoming syrup in spring air,
and in the bottom of the pan. Stirring
constantly in turn: mother, father, son.
We disagree about when it's done
aproning just right to breakfast
pancakes, to pour in cold glass to store
for all our guests, "the knowing" we call
them. Those that recognize necessities
found in the heart of every day.

The Recluse at Ma's Café

The waitresses know me here
and count me in their orders to Ma.
I wear my straw hat low over my eyes
so that the other customers
can't look in.
They don't need to know
a thing about me.
Save that I take my coffee
black and that the last
time I came to town
there was a foot of snow
on the ground.
If the truth be known,
even as I sit here
I wish for home.
The cornfields
and the pastures
I know like the back
of my hand.
I can feel somehow
the Holsteins
in the south pasture
eating grass,
and I need their company
more than the company of men.
The cows are not so noisy
or so eager
to make me feel
out of place.
A marsh hawk circles
even now
in the air above them.
The fading glow
of evening

will find me in
the barn; a polka on the radio
lightens my step
from one cow to the next.
I go between them, smiling,
happily at home.

Least Resistance

(2007)

Reminders

Remind me, love, of what is missing
of how the troubled sky is just
a sky observed by one with a troubled heart.
Remind me of that time before the storm
when the air smelled of lilacs and daffodils.
Name the stars for me on a summer night.
Tell me their stories like the progress
of a dream. Name tunes we once danced
to in the early winter around the fire
as we traced a path in the fiery embers
of maple, oak, and birch.

I know it's not the love I have forgotten,
and not the stars I wished on as a child
or the fireflies in the jar near my bed
or your hands telling the story of our
time together forming the shape of life
within the memory of love. Love
that remains both near and distant
at the same instant.

Sidewalk Sweeper: Mann's Chinese Theater

I am composed of dust and air
and the constant blood that runs
in circles from head to foot.
My hands grip this broom. Its
bristles work like a glacier on earth
and in a million years all this
will be erased like a chalk board
wiped clean, and well before that,
I will certainly be dust beneath the feet.
But for now, I sweep in clear
light. Sweep clear these prints
primitive signatures locked in
cement. This light leaves me
happy at the thought of thinking these
thoughts. Sweeping here. The work
I do each morning to greet
the day.

Traffic is suspended between
red and green. The newsstand down
the street bundles terror against
the darkness. My feet are mired
in the footprints of stars. Their hands
grip these bristles then let go. And if
I could I would fly in the air like dust
circle in updrafts and soar so far
away — rising upward and widening
out.

Throwing Shot Put
For Fergus 2004

Let's gather together in the middle
Of a world of circles and spheres;
Heavenly, with disks and roundness —
The preferred shape of the universe —
All sharp edges honed by sand and stone
Until shiny. Honed by gravity itself,
And time. Moving like the galaxy moves,
Outward in all directions at once.
Or forward: the direction you are
Facing at the time. So much to balance
And in turn so hard to balance
What is round.
                   What a chance you take just stepping
Into the circle, becoming as you do it, the center
Of something because of your place in it:
Like life. Declare this round world home
Or house or holy or any other round word .
Expire breath out into air along the lines
That must not be crossed; the answer to all
Questions held deep within a round heart.

Photo Left on the Copy Machine

Just before the storm,
as the hollyhock by the back
window struggled to outdo itself
this year growing, for once, taller
than the first pane of the south
window. Lowell and Marge posed
by the back step. It was Tuesday
and Blackie, the dog, was back
from the neighbors for once.
Marge stands solid,
her hair back off her face
in the heat, and Lowell's arms
tan from outdoor work
are gently around her waist.
Her own pale hands are on
his more for the sake of modesty
than shadowy desire. Their
hearts each hold
separate wishes made up of equal
parts hope and good weather.
They didn't know that the bicycle
that night would circle in a funnel
of topsoil and be found three miles
from town. Or that the house
would dematerialize except
for the kitchen table and its
bouquet of poppies in a glass vase
standing in the middle of a lace
table cloth, the walls all disappeared.
Or that straw would stand
embedded like tiny spears
in the light pole back by the barn.
In future photos the smile
on each face is tentative, uprooted

like the lilacs, and turned, like the old
Schwinn, upside down. "That's it,"
the photographer whispered, "Now smile,"
and they obeyed.

Police Report: A Found Poem

A citizen
Reported a moose
On highway forty-five.
Upon further investigation
The moose
Turned out to be
A donkey
Missing one leg.

Irezumi

"Just as westerners donate their organs after death, a Japanese wearing the work of a grand tattoo master may donate his skin to a museum or university. Tokyo University has three hundred such masterpieces framed."
— Diane Ackerman, *A Natural History of the Senses*

Sew me down. Bind me to ink and needle
Through all time. Let me remove my clothes
And drink the garish liquor of my
Body created anew. The legend in image
That spreads across my chest. A dragon
Whose eye becomes a part of me. It must
Hug my flesh until it infuses itself
Into my quaking being — blood in my blood.
But what is creation's price if not pain?
How can one avoid the hurt that comes
As a sad sister to the master's art?
I cried when that eye was rendered
Its rich pupil touches my heart and reflects
That pain. It looks in and out at the same time.
This chest, this stomach, see how the curve
Of it is lost in rich half tones? The delicacy
Reminded the artist of a young boy
And here he is, on my side, joining me forever
As I become text – mythic by composition.
This skin is no more mine than I will be
A man after my death, but I will live
Forever. My purpose, at least, will forever
Live – live to be a story in ink and color.
The dead display of my best parts framed
Without me. Turning out to be
More image than man.

Passport Photograph

In the background there should be smoke,
And mountains, and in this light, a falcon
Racing the wind to an imaginary border.

There should be an untidy city street
Filled with the smell of sweat and spice;
Spider webs trailing from windowsills,
And the sound of an old man coughing
In the dark.
                Somewhere the sound of footsteps,
Too, treading on the empty edge of fear.
They stop when I do. Perhaps an echo
That in daylight would be eaten up
By men in dark coats, but at night lingers
Leaving tracks in the sound darkness makes.

There should be dark women too
With heavy eyelids that whisper in a language
I can't begin to understand threatening
And comforting at the same time.
Alone with these thoughts I think more
And give this country a name.

Telling the Bees

"This tradition, once prevalent in Central Europe, British Isles, and North America, mandates that beekeepers must inform their bees of important family events. To fail in these communications might mean an infant would die or a marriage dissolve." – Elizabeth Atwood, from the essay 'The Sacred Bee ,The Filthy Pig, and the Bat Out of Hell: Animal Symbolism as Cognative Biophilia'

Here we are. This gathering darkness edges
Our grove of honeysuckle, honey locust,
Burning bush – still secrets opening to a dream.
You will know my life, I promise, a covenant
Between us. You know my wife? Her body
Swells escaping itself in the laughter
Of children. She tells me there is nothing
Sweeter than the tired breath of them
Dreaming in another room. I disagree,
But still I wish I could dream. My sleep
Is unpeopled.

All right, to be honest, once
I dreamed.

It was winter. Your hives were covered with bits
Of my old clothing so you would feel warm.
So you would remember I was still alive
Those long winter months and not swarm
Away. It was morning in the dream
And the woman that owns the farm across
The clover was hanging laundry. Her eyes
Are the richest green and her hair tangles
Like downy locust below her shoulders.
She is as beautiful as a meadow opening
To sunshine. There was a hint of wisteria

On the breeze.
I've told you I give her honey.
It began to rain. I helped her gather laundry
From the line: some shirts, an old quilt.
We laughed: at rain, at ourselves, and sat
In her kitchen. She was baking bread. It smelled.
The whole world smelled of baking bread.
She opened the honey and dipped her finger
In. The honey ribboned back on itself. Then
She placed her finger on my lips. In the dream,
I was beside myself, or above myself really,
Watching it all unfold and being part of it too.
I loved her then and dripped fresh honey
On her shoulder, kissed it away, thinking
Which is sweeter and in what way? Her mouth,
Her neck just below her ear, were worlds
Opening to other worlds. Were calm days
Clear with no wind; perfect flying weather.
The children woke me. Sneaking to surround
My bed and shout me into day: I'll will you
To those children when I die.
But here we are.
The sun is slipping past birch and sumac.
One of you is circling me like a dying
Planet or a dream unfolding. I've gone on too
Long, but our agreement holds. You will
Know first, in the quiet hours of evening,
All the private orbit of my life. The clumsy
Dance of everyday: my inability to dream.

New Pens and a School Project at the Lower Sioux Agency

An eagle drifts in thermals
teasing updrafts above the river.
The sap is running against winter
an act of faith for late February,
and my son, amazed, sees a grasshopper
bound off the trail. He catches it in
his hand and it balances for a second
on his thumb, like we balance between
the eagle and the running blue river.
It's bright green in sunlight and leaps
to bluestem the color of autumn.
        All this seems
like a dream of August. A dream
from the past when warriors decided
it was a good day to die.
      We arrive
at the opposite conclusion and decide
it is a good day to live; so we do.
As if the choice were ours alone.
The eagle swirls above us and
the river unravels secrets on the valley
floor. We hang-fire somewhere
between the two with new pens to order
this unruly world with words,
like the river orders the map
in unexpected lines on paper. We
manage an equal truth in letters
on the landscape of our hearts.
The eagle banks downwind:
out of sight.

After Reading Octavio Paz I go Fish Walleyes in the Minnesota River

"The great night swift over your body." – Octavio Paz

What brings me here, alone,
To cast a line in this muddy water?
To look at me, standing
On this slab of crystalline bedrock
Three billion years old,
One wouldn't think I was dying.
The game warden didn't think so
When he stopped on the bridge
Above me to shoot the breeze.
The walleyes that take my jig
Every few casts only know "now"
As it fades into the next season: winter.
I release them. I've lost the desire
To kill anything, so everything
Comes to me already dead.
The sun is escaping toward evening.
I stare at its setting until
My vision explodes in color:
I save those colors against the great night.
There is music in the water
Over rocks gathering itself
In foam. And in the wood ducks
That blast through trees
Downstream; urgent as the need
To embrace loneliness like their wings
Embrace autumn air,
A still life of unfair passing.
If this scene were a painting,
I would be almost invisible.
The trees, oak, elm, willow,
Would fill the frame. Then rock.

Then water. I would become nothing
As I decline toward nothing.
It is darker now.
On the way to the car,
One deer stands in wheat stubble,
It glows red in the last light of day
Undisturbed by my quiet passing
Down wind.

Conversation with a Girl Sculpting a Fist: Faribault Area Learning Center

With the nightly news as a background
and as if I am not there, you say when you
were growing up there was never money
for food.
Your fingers are creating
fingers, creating veins on a wrist and then
knuckles: like saying to your mother
"I'll be right there." But instead
you say, "This war. There is a darkness
that will last my whole life. Killing
is killing it doesn't matter who is doing
it or why."
                      The evening news shows a boy
not much older than you coming home
from war, and in the shadow behind him
there is the darkness he brings home
with him, and that you must live with.
And your sister
had to move to Arizona and you
miss her, you say, so much, because for years
it was just the two of you. And in summers
when the power died in the dark heart
of a thunderstorm, you sisters hugged
each other on the living room floor.
The name, you said, gave you hope.
Surrounded in the darkness by a circle
of flashlights gathered all day against
the news of bad weather.
The fist is a fist now.
Tomorrow, you say, when it is fired,
you hope it won't explode.

Priming the Pump

Aspen toss their leaves to the wind.
We are thirsty from walking all this way
and come upon a solitary pump
standing like a monument
in the cramped clearing of an
abandoned farm grove. The dogs,
those simple creatures, close their eyes
to dissipate the heat by making it disappear
with invisibility. Our meager water bottle
is magnified in meagerness by the potential
flood beneath our feet, so my son
absently pumps the handle
looks into the spout and pumps again.
There are spider webs where water
should be, but water begets water
and we take a chance pouring ours
into the pump shaft and hoping
it creates a seal to draw the water up.
And for awhile we pump in disbelief.
The sound of rust repeated in the song
of Sandhill Cranes heading south
across the sky. The pumping
changes then and water spills as red
with rust as blood, and floods upon
the concrete apron. Then with further
pumping clears. The dogs drink
in rivulets that form along the ground
and we drink too, in turn, one pumping
water out. Water so perfect it becomes
what water is to us. All water will be
compared to this for ever after.
                                        We've
been there since. And walked that wood
in search of woodcock and ruffed grouse,

But we never found that pump again.
The trees never were the same. The path that
took us there has disappeared with compass
and with map we failed to find our way
back until forward was the only way
to go and we walk on alone but filled with hope.

I Close The Door

I close the door
not a figurative door, a real one
shipped here from a warehouse in Chicago.
I have waited all night in a chair for my
father to die. They turned off the monitors
that stay attached but no longer blip
or flash in the dark. They are saving me
the trouble of watching the struggle of life
beating and missing within him:
turned off the monitors for me, really,
I know the signals are being sent
to the other room. And I know
as he resists this passing — a full moon
over the millpond out the window —
that he's hung on so long he's forgotten
how to let go. So I tell him with words,
"You can let go now." And the long night
passes. The night nurse sits with me
for awhile and we talk about what he
knows, what he feels, what he hears.
I hold his hand hoping to dissolve
the emptiness we each must step into alone.
His breath so shallow I imagine sea
shells appearing in the sand so shallow
a butterfly could pass and fail to notice
breath at all. And as sunlight pinks
the horizon — like going to work —
he dies. I stand up then at his bedside
the shift has changed and a new nurse
opens the door I look at her and say,
"I know," and she says something
to eliminate a confusion that never existed.
A car honks at nothing out on the street,
a pigeon banks into the sun,
I close the door.

In Shadows

We grow so large the world misses
a beat trying to contain us. The clock
we live by whether we admit it or not,
swallows whole streets, and the dog
dances with itself in the setting
sunlight; just before nightfall, it tries
to catch up with its shadow, with night.

And in the dark, we imagine the shadow
all objects cast . The crater a bomb makes
in the sand. The water each dying tongue
hopes for at the last. Shadows do not
make happy poems; do not attend luncheons.
They do not weather the fronts crossing
a troubled heart, but when shadows
close in on all we hold dear, or know
in our hearts to be true, we grow bigger
with each passing breath until we nearly
become the air, the water, the light
or dark. We become the other self
featureless in shadows and grace. And
in becoming our fullest, we are tempted
to abandon this world and go off
into the other country or into the sky
casting a giant shadow backward to earth
with our own thoughts holding us down.
The unthinkable one measure of our days.

Maple and Fir

If I said the noise of the stars
at night kept me from sleeping
you would assume that some dark
craziness had descended on me.
Or at least the fear of that darkness
moving so quickly it makes a sound
like wind at night over water in waves
or the same wind through maple and fir.
Instead, I wonder how it is you don't
hear it? I've tried through these
long nights to see it as a gift. To transpose
it from curse to revelation, like stepping
on stones to cross the smallest stream,
but it doesn't work. There's just
insistent humming and darkness
and the vague encouragement of so
many tiny lights spinning: weaving
the seasons. Winter is worst, but then
I light a fire and hear the crackling
that signals all is well. Before long
sunlight pinks the horizon in the east
and the quiet daylight comes round again.
And the sudden stars come quietly to rest.

The Water Witch

Mother says
it began with a dream
at seven.
Be that as it may
to this day
I imagine myself a child
held out to a thunderstorm.
A gift, my mother calls it,
but I know it is less a gift
and more an inclination.
I incline toward water
pure and simple,
deep and cool.
My blood somehow translates
the secrets of seepage
shifts in geography
as subtle as the way
some tell weather by the morning
clouds. I take a spring cut apple bough
forked
one branch in each hand
and walk.
The feeling I get
here in the chest
is what could most be called a gift.
And after,
when the circle is scratched
in the dust
and the farmer offers a cold drink,
as he always does,
I tell him no.
Water, or the sense of water,
fills me up.
If the farmer has a child

it will look at me and cry.
They all do.
I am accustomed to it,
which may be why I never married.
Mother says it's because
I'm set in my ways:
the ways of water.
As for religion,
I don't need it.
I have the creek behind the house
and the willow tree for shade.
The Lutheran farmers
around here will tell you
God is stingy with his presents
and giving away whole days
to water
is trying business.
I need my tea
a bath
and the cool grass under
that willow tree
where I'm free to dream of rivers rising
and sense the silent tug
of a full moon.

After Reading Tu Fu I Go Off To Catch Rough Fish In the Cannon River

The river carries off the moon
To set beyond the border.
— Tu Fu

Together, carp gather like shadows in the slack
current, moving like dark thoughts through
the moon's shadow. We are joined by a line
the exact thickness of desire: a line that stretches
into current moving below the surface in ways
only the moon understands; pulled by its fullness
to extremes that become more than only the Cannon
River. That become all rivers stretching the borders
of what I know for a fact to be true. In the settling
darkness: me, the moon, this carp all balance on
the sudden edge of daylight and dark. All the while,
doing my best to stay connected. When the fish
comes to hand in the shallows, offering itself
like the answer to some question that I don't
recall asking, I handle it gently. Then let it go.

After Drinking with Friends I Write a Poem While Walking Home

The glorious parking lot illuminated
by streetlights and moonbeams; small
shards of broken glass like flotsam
between painted lines that create order
from darkness like the banks of a river.
A train disappears into the dark
but my feet still detect its passing
like the sound of time itself going
off into some other eternity.
Could one wish for more from a night
spent drinking with friends? More, I mean,
than stars repeated in broken glass
and the great locomotive passing
at just the instant I step into the dark.

October: Kewauni River

There are so many symbols here for me
to ignore. The river itself a line
on the map disappearing in green.
In real life it's low with autumn. The leaves
turn and fall. Salmon are dead along
the shore or fining their way upstream
to spawn then die. Even the sky
is low and drizzles on a town that smells
of metal being worked.   It's no surprise
that I feel a lightness in this world;
a joy that borders on giddiness as I
eat eggs, potatoes, and meat at 5 A.M.
The secret, I believe, is staying connected
not as simple as it appears these days,
and to convince salmon that are not
eating to eat the streamer as it swings
past them on its way back to me. If I do
my part I feel their life connect with mine
for awhile.   It's the thin line racing
any way it desires, creating
the narrowest margin in the quiet forest. I
follow the fish where it leads charging
upstream. I lose it occasionally around
a bend or watch it leap high as I bow
to give it slack and let it fall. There
is a bit of sunlight in the late afternoon
I feel the warmth on my back. Other fish
run like a river in reverse: geese crisscross
the sky, a leaf disappears in a riffle, and I
measure my heart as it beats in my chest.

A Magician Daydreams

I will make something
From thin air
Starting small
And working up to magic.
I could make you disappear
But choose not to
Choose instead a mood
And a deck of cards
All changed to hearts.
Choose knotted,
Brightly colored, silk scarves
From my empty palm,
Choose coins from thin air.
This sleight of hand
A warm-up for later,
And as sleeves grow empty
I get smaller,
Real magic
Depends on that.
Doves from a cape
And my fingers fly
More beautiful in part
Than the whole of me
Always on the edge of your
World.
A rabbit from a top hat,
A cane turned to a bouquet:
I am shrinking to nothing.
Tonight I will sleep
Alone, barely visible,
Conjuring images of you
With my right hand
Dreaming audience and applause
Magic of their own

As dependable
As trap doors
False bottoms
And mirrors.

The Magician's Assistant

At one time
We loved doing magic together.
For all those years
He directed our illusions.
To be honest, it hurt.
I was the one
That had to fit into the damned
Things. Then move,
Gracefully as any dancer,
In those tight spaces
As he locks locks
And opens tiny doors
To reveal my parts to the crowd
All just to make himself look good.

Imagine yourself
Being sawed in half
And trying to look happy about it.
Or imagine being
In that wicker basket
Him standing above you
With a fist full of swords
Sharp enough to shave with
Ready to run you through,
And he's smiling.
I gaze up in the dark basket just then
And look for a flash of light
On the very tip of the blade
As it peaks through
The wicker like the illusion
That anything is possible.
I grab the blade
And pull it down hard.
I do the trick for god's sake

Not him.
Some nights I make believe
I'm the illusion
Misty as lace tossed
By stage light.
He assists me
On those nights.
I rise weightless as smoke
To disappear,
Then rematerialize
As someone else
In someone else's life.

In Praise of Frogs

"After the Maggid's death his disciples came together and talked about the things he had done. When it was Rabbi Schneur Zalman's turn; he asked them: 'Do you know why our master went to the pond every day at dawn and stayed there for awhile before coming home again?' They did not know why. Rabbi Zalman continued: 'He was learning the song with which the frogs praise God. It takes a long time to learn that song.'"
– *Tales of Hasidim: Early Masters* Retold by Martin Buber.

After, as it turns out, a lifetime
Of mornings, with the fog hugging
Close to the swamp, and a pond lily
Quivering in the first morning breeze
With the sun half risen, orange
Above the cedars, and the lonely breath
Of dawn chilling right through
My clothes, I lingered a bit.
To be honest, I lingered a life.
My hair going from black
To gray. I listened patiently,
Really listened, to the song of frogs
Their song, building, first one brave soul
Then an unlikely chorus, rising,
Until silenced by the sun
As it turned from orange to yellow,
Dawn into day. At first I thought
That no one knew where I was those
Mornings. I persisted in that belief for years.
Even though I returned with mud between
My toes and the smell of cedar about me.
They'll say I returned knowing
The song the frogs sing to praise God.
It makes a nice story, but I ask you,

Am I the type to think a thing
Like that? No, it is the world
I learned to praise from frogs. From frogs
I learned there is only faith. The delicate
Balancing act of every day — the sky tilting
Above – the water and earth below.
To balance well was to feel the magic
That holds the stars in place.
To balance well on this world is praise.
The frogs give voice to dragonfly
To flat lily. They make me understand
That the word for teaching and the word
For learning is the same word.
But the frogs just sang
Frog songs in breaking light.
And if there is a God he lives
In a frog's belly, touching the same mud
From which I crawled millenniums ago.
I praise the God of frogs that took
My own kind of forever to understand.

Waiting for all the Rest

The sun in some east is waiting
even as it rises there. The ocean
too is waiting for the moon that is
waiting to be full. Full enough
to exert a tug along the ocean's
watery course.
                        The salmon are waiting
to return, as the stream in its
watery depths and drastic pools
gathers waiting to be what salmon
recognize as home. The kingfisher
is waiting to transform fish into bird
waiting above water
                              until the right
moment, then waiting more,
and the eastern sun and the night
together wait to create a day. Waiting
to create a whole, and the air is waiting
to be inspired, then waiting to exhale
out to the waiting world. Waiting
for the sun to rise again like the human
breast rises, waiting for another morning
another night, waiting for all the rest.

Stone & Sky

(2011)

On the Border

My home is on the border between dark
and light, between this country
and the other world. I live
in language. My home
is perched between sea and shore
the same border that separates
one from the other. Living here
is like living there, but in important
ways it is different. Different here
in the heart of all that borders other
than the heart. My home is on
the border, the contact zone, where
things mix as they struggle to remain
separate. Where love joins its opposite.
Where clouds race, and the wind
crosses with indifference like the space
between strings on a black guitar.
A melody machined from the harvest
of wheat along lines that we only
imagine. The borderland, the frontier,
the first step where I begin my climb,
thicket and field, hope and what
remains when hope crosses over
to become something else.

Reminder: Friday Night

If ever I needed a reminder that we
Are all fallen members of a lost
Tribe, it is today when work is done,
And the air crackles with electricity.

I imagine myself lighter somehow,
In all this, the dancer I never was, smoky,
And unsaved against a backdrop
Of ink and ashes. All week has lead

To this night, and the certainty
I will fail again to inhale the smoldering
Scent of salvation; a hell
Of its own it seems. I prefer the words

Of St. Catherine of Siena who said,
"All the way to heaven is heaven."
Perhaps she will appear from behind
The bandstand and perhaps we will dance

Creating our own heaven step by step
Our own earthly salvation, our own text.

Poem with a Line from Tom McGrath

In this pasture the bulls have
put rings in their noses
and the coyotes wear crowns of asphodels.
In this pasture the bees fly to flowers
in formation as accidental as pollination
itself giving rise to a whole universe
of bee worlds. In this pasture a man
on a folding chair plays guitar
to the mower; a sweet song with whole
notes like clover. In this pasture
the bulls have put rings in their
noses and paw in soft dirt
a welcome and a warning
with the same graceful hoof.

Mouse

I switch off the yard light
and the stars emerge
from shadows like mice around
a granary. They reason in dark
corners and scamper
on the edge of vision like tiny
meteors trail light
toward the horizon until light blinks
out.
      In the darkness these
creatures give meaning
to ambiguity. And
death like light also comes from above
in the noiseless whisper of an owl.
Questioning. But what is the question
anyway? Is it about day
breaking hours from now? Or about
dreams I've been having lately
figuratively filled with people
just like me that disappear in light.
"Think something," I say to myself
and wander off to bed.

Firewood
For Fergus

Always the blue sky above
Our heads, and the grass green
Beneath our feet, and the autumn
Parade of geese noisily passing
Ordered like words on the page.
But back then you, Fergus, were
Just ten, and you set the wedge
Where the splitting maul and my
Might failed to split the maple
Into wood. No need to make comparison
Between that failure and all my others.
No need then to draw conclusions
Because we had that future
Spread out before us like an endless
Autumn of blue clear skies, and geese
Passing, and grass beneath our feet.
But today, all these years later,
I'm alone out back splitting another
Maple. The sky blue and you surprisingly
Appear in the doorway almost
Filling it, and set about helping me
Again. Lifting whole branches
In place to be cut moving like
I imagine a young god must move
In some ancient story of redemption.
And we work like this for awhile
Shoulder to shoulder, step for step,
Father and son.
Creating what will warm this
House some winter years from now,
And we remain
Twice warmed like the old men
Say of making wood. And my heart

Joins the geese high above our
Heads then returns to earth as all
Our lofty thought must do
To this earth tangled with roots
And littered as it is with saw dust
Good enough for another day.

Where the Bones

Where the bones come out of the earth,
at the intersection of longing and desire;
they don't look like bones at all at first,
but on closer examination they measure
the stories we hope to tell in some future.
They embolden lightness like leaves
tossed by wind against sunshine.
Where bones come out of the earth,
all the stories are possible. All characters
are you like in a dream. Flesh is not
necessary for the imagination. It is superfluous.
It is unintended like a sudden rain —
the accident of atmosphere – the way
water seeks a path of least resistance
down the valley. An accident of gravity
and whiteness, and the dark passages
where bones come out of the earth,
and sing bone songs, hard, and strong, and bright.

Two in Love

There was no noise and little light.
The wind dodged down
the road like a small bird.
A heart fluttered within itself,
and the brain made up a story
that involved mirrors and something
that really wasn't there.

What is the world of two in love?
All curses and exclamations. Why
crave sleep, or lightning, or rocks
the way an old man craves the moments
of his youth.

Why resist the inroads love makes.
Heart on heart, eyes look into eyes,
and the mind spins old stories
about quiet times with little
wind along empty roads. In love
with invention as one who looks down
a well then listens for a pebble
rippling in the darkness like
two in love.

Gratitude

Whisper of it in dark corners
and mumble what passes for a prayer.
Build small monuments against
despair – make them of sunlight
and clover. Let deer nibble their edges
and fill themselves for now.
Then remember a perfect story
and draw with it a picture, an image,
of stone, and sky, and fire.
A truck shifts down the street
bringing with it a moment of clear
interruption before gratitude spirals
back into trees, darkness, and silence.
Preparing for the day ahead to appear,
it seems, out of nowhere
like bird song or a slight wind.

Writing with a New Pen, I Recall The Old Chinese Poets

The loneliness of raindrops in a dirty puddle
Skipped over on the way to buy cigarettes at Super America.

Those old Chinese poets that always see the world
Doubled in some sort of parallel reflection.

They never need a Marlboro bad as heroin
A drug introverts take these days breathing

Its dragon smoke deep into their shy lungs
And later, after a few months, the needle

More solid than air slamming it into the blood
Mixing with their very soul – their heart

Their brain, a needle tracing veins back
To the source. Becoming two things

The drug and the heart. The drug
And the brain. The drug against reflection

Of any puddle. The prick in flesh like a match
Lighted illuminating desire. I think, I'm glad

I never started smoking – I mean – because
I know I could never stop. The raindrops

In a puddle – it must be said –because I looked
Reflect, a light pole, a Buick, the curb, my shoes.

The only way to look is down. The old
Chinese poets know that puddles aren't

Reflecting anything that could possibly be
Mistaken for an answer. That's it;

Just smoke curling like bus exhaust,
On seventh street, in early November.

Tired of What Is Beautiful

Three deer slowly eat their way
Through the garden. The Cooper's
Hawk glares at me from a low branch.
Its eyes describe contempt for any creature
Incapable of flight. I sit here watching
For so long this afternoon
I feel I might blossom. The truth
Remains hidden in time as it passes.
In the shade that moves
With the sun measuring nothing
That matters to the deer
Or the hawk, or the basswood,
Or me. I'm sorry is all I can think
To say, sorry.

On Endings

The long slope of her thigh
Along the shade from
A passing cloud, pushing
Sunshine aside for flesh
And wind. The touch of a hand
Like a spider's web
Explores itself and discovers
What is already captured by air.
In the taste that hints at flesh
The source
Of everything hidden in these moments
Passing quietly into forever.
Will they ever circle back to now?
Or will they orbit past flesh
And into some deeper air.

What September Means

September has its own deep scent; memories
That return all on their own hesitating
Like summer hesitates for a moment here.
Then, like a pen that runs out of ink
In the middle of this line, is replaced by
Something bolder like autumn. More
Sudden, more severe, like a sparrow
Hitting the window. Small things recalled
Alone, not cheerful exactly, but not sad
Either, just nameable as memory. As fish,
Bewildered by current, head downstream
Before disappearing like the path each
Day takes floating into night. Not meaning
Any one thing until returned to later and
Perhaps not meaning anything even then.

Stone and Sky

Take away the stone and what
Remains? Just the nature of it
Ringing in dark circles all night
Hosting fire and dust. The same
Dust that calls us by name
Into eternity to join it.

And sky — sky is our only hope
For what will pass as salvation.
It is the vessel eternity escapes
Into. A hollow world filled only
With whispers and sunset. The stone
And sky resolve to separate forever,

But the thin line of the horizon
Reveals their collaboration is an illusion
Of distance. The sweet soft song of time.
Looking there our eyes encompass both
Stone and sky becoming forever
Stone and sky hearth and firelight.

The Initiation of Praise

2014

My Reader

My reader is part of a small
club like those who fancy
terriers and the taking of game
to ground. My reader stumbled
on this book by accident because
of a mistransposed order
number or an absent minded
librarian that was thinking
about fishing instead of listening
at the time. My reader curls
on the couch by a dog. My reader
holds a glass of something
that has some grief in it,
and folds the book
back on itself breaking the binding
like day breaks in the east
orange then yellow. My reader
smells of dew and wild mint,
and can keep a secret, and knows
at least two good lawyers.
My reader is not sensitive; believes
in big foot and not the Loch Ness
monster. My reader's favorite
North American ungulate
is the Musk Ox. My reader
dreams of flying, dreams of vessels
of containment, dreams
of more poems like this one.

The Table

On the table I place the contents
of my pocket. Sixty-three dollars,
keys that open my house; a list
of what needs to be done.
I place my son on the table
and the troubling solitude
of each day. He's right next to the reflection
of time, that doesn't travel well,
that floats and spins in gloom,
hung up at last on the back of an old chair,
like a ragged sweater,
used now only for warmth.

I place next
to the vase of flowers, a token
of my own ruin. A shadow
taken from my father's garden
when I was just a boy, and he
was as strong as any God;
a shadow, and next to it,
I set an unexplained amalgamation
of hope.

Carp

Carp school in slack current
like deer bunch up
along the edge of a wood in the evening
or like a cottontail in its form
waits all day.
They mill about and
change position swinging wide
as if eternally thinking
about a difficult problem.
The current sweeps past them
like a wind. Like the way time
sweeps past as words and actions
and errors sweep past a life. Resistance
is barely noticeable. The sun rises
and sets on golden scales. They sink
back to deeper water to wait
for the seasons to turn,
for another full moon, for that
something only carp
can completely understand.

Ground Nesting

When we met it seemed we whistled
The song of the meadow lark. A bird
You had forgotten even though as a child
They sounded from every road ditch
And fence post. But now at twenty-one
Driving down a South Dakota road
You ask me "What is that bird, yellow
Breast, black V?" "A meadow lark," I
Respond. A brightness crosses your face
Like a memory of something from a deep
Past – an infant hearing the music infants
Hear. And now that ghost of the prairie
In your past is coming back to you.
On the phone you talk about the wind
Like you would talk about a character
From a Russian novel who eats only
Black bread and nettle soup. And in
Person your eyes gaze off at the horizon
Into a distance that defines "far" like
A hawk's eyes; they see the slightest
Movement, a fat mouse in switch
Grass, a nest with a clutch of eggs
Nestled in sweet clover, like a knitted
Hat nestled against your hair
And beard in a silence that isn't silence;
A silence that instead just is.

Jubilee

We were young men
with stones for eyes, but what
did it matter? We stared into the darkness
anyway.
           We were ripe — softening
like grapes left too long
on the vine. Our ears were open though
searching
         as if for the sound
of something ringing, hammer on anvil
perhaps, in the darkness, like a shiver.
Now the world
              grows less clear each day
but the ferns and the jack-in-the-pulpit
hold to their plan. So does heat lightning
along
      the horizon and sunrise.
We remain we. In praise for Saturday
morning — for stones and for lightning
that strikes no one.

Before Stepping

"The words stop but the meaning keeps going on."
— Basho

Let it be the moment
before stepping into the water to fish.
Flies lined up in a box like
days on a calendar. A cigar
still unlit waiting: cows,
the definition of bliss, graze along
the far bank like those things
in life we hope to never forget.
Be there in that moment.
Just before water presses and
chills against legs. The gentle
pressure of time passing.
Wait a moment and study rocks
or insect wings diaphanous as the skin
on a girl's wrist, and the sky
so blue: and high, and clear,
and bright. Let it be the moment
before stepping off the bank
from solid ground to gravel
and sand, and the muck we originally
crawled out of into a new world
that contains our better self. And
let that world last for our
own particular kind of forever.

Digging Post Holes

It is the digging, and the taking
away of dirt, that is my first love.
The solemn pile of soil climbing
beside the hole, and the revelation
of the passing layers: topsoil, rock,
sand and clay. The harmony of colors
shifting like a secret. Occasionally a gift
tree root, or a perfect round black
rock suggests some primitive
tool. It is the progress of going
deeply to ground.
The moistness spilling
up like scent with each lift of the digger
the gripping and letting go
of the small measures that pass
for progress, down below the
frost line, into the continuity
of earth. Unaffected by what
is above, the heaving of my breath,
the pulse threading through my
body, the sunshine over my shoulder,
like hope, spills into the darkness
illuminating the once still earth.

Sweat Lodge: Morton, Minnesota

It is framed with long river willow
and hung over with blankets blocking
out the orbit of the night sky, the cold,
the autumn air. Coals glow like hungry eyes
in the darkness. Then hiss the first rush
of wet white heat. The breath of deep
in the earth – the center of all this.
Faces only barely visible each creating
its own world inhabited by creatures
we love or fear.
                    Time is suspended
like a cottonwood seed on an errant
breeze. It stops being seed, stops being
time, and becomes water and smoke
and darkness. Thinking evaporates.
Boundaries stretch outward. Together.
Alone. No wind. One lone feather
trembles – speaking a language
I don't understand.

My Blood

My blood is beating in my ears
Like water drawn up through
Sunken roots deep in the ground.

Corn stubble stretches to the horizon
Constructing the geography of now
The field mouse burrows in a dead furrow,

And I take the first step of a long journey.
The initiation of praise. The start
Of a new path through an old world.

"Hold nothing back," I think to myself
And know, despite my best efforts,
Today is simply like any other day.

The Stroke

Here the streetlights stay on
past daybreak and the wind
brings the smell of bacon
cooking in the house down
the street. Next door, a child
wheezes at the ceiling. Outside,
in the back yard, I consider
the dogs as they explore the dew.
They circle each other as they
circle the yard – orbits within
orbits – never touching. It is not
a dream although it appears it
might be one. I can see my own
hand when I raise it, and the sound,
one Cardinal repeating itself,
is as clear as if the Cardinal, too,
lived somewhere in my head
emerging now as music. Do
dreams contain smells? I don't
think so. I resolve to move
forward with the day
seeing everything all at once
like a painting.

Just Outside Aberdeen, South Dakota

In my mind, I track ducks
In astonishing numbers as they circle a marsh
North of town: mallards, ring-necks, canvas backs,
Teal. They circle and spin in great dark orbits
Searching the cattails for safe passage.
And the wind, like a creature from the north,
Fuels their need to land, or failing that
Continue south all night and out of state.
Round bales stretch to the horizon
Like monuments from some ancient
Civilization that, no doubt, worshipped
Wheat.
In my mind, evening is coming on.
The dog whimpers in the cold. She senses
The urge to migrate too an urge that's
New to her today, an urge to wander
The countryside, to go feral, to desert me
To fend for herself, take her chances
With the landscape, fight her way through it
And float upward until she becomes an idea.
We are not alone here on the edge of thought
We are doubled. Like sky in marsh water
Like duck bellies on the surface of the sky,
And in my mind, one mallard tail feather
Curly as a northern low drifts to the water
Like a pendulum back and forth
Back and forth until it lands — floating here
Buoyant as hope in the face of loss.

Still

The mirror
like the still water
only knows the language
of light. At sunset,
when the long-tailed weasel
sets out to feast,
and the cold snow
squeaks in response,
if one listens closely,
it sounds like starlight.
I understand the wandering
cold. The nature of dark
wishes that come true
simply because they
are wishes, and they must.
Through this cold night
the dogs chase in their
sleep. Through the icy
cold I whisper what I
once knew of love.
Under the mirror
of the lake, carp feed.
They tug at water
in light fading
like a hunger
still.

The Lie

Bold designs that learn the hard way.
Designs with less substance than a butterfly's
Wing — a signature of solid gold —
Gilded ownership. Own it with words
To spare. A concentric circle of desirable
Outcomes none of them really there.
Like a wind, like a barometer rising.
The pressure to build one upon the other
Until lies compete like smoke, like darkness,
Like a whisper. In the brightest light
On the darkest corner, incomplete.
Something missing, the details of venom
In the teeth of a great snake.
Flowers refuse to blossom and
Promises break like heart ache.

Simulacrum

Sunlight trickles through basswood
and comes to rest like a spirit on water
patching it in light and shadow.
A minnow, grateful the blue heron
was frightened into the air,
returns to lip an agate in the shallows.
A leatherback turtle, up for air,
floats downstream. My eye
meets his eye, and he dives deeper
disappearing in a clear green pool.
We are all here, and up to now, singular.
No community of the commons. No
understanding of one another aside
from what is on the surface
obvious to sunlight and
each obvious to itself as it is.

Ambition

The moon and Venus
blink at each other
believing, I imagine,
in their place in the May
sky. My wife says,
"Sit here on the edge
of the bed — see there
is the moon — and over
there Venus." Sure
enough the moon
still beams through
the just still dark
and Venus, through
maple boughs, winks.
Time is passing as it
always has. We touch
hands, and for one
moment in that time
lives perfection.

Smelt Run

The evening flood is a tributary
Of darkness. Water reflects
Stars and moon like those things
That only exist in the night.
My net searches moonlight
And shadow. In between time
Smelt like silver coins spill
Upstream. And I remain a sinner,
Still unrepentant, still wagering
The profits of sin.
                    I dip into
The sky and carry silver questions
To shore. Frighten me with headlights
Running through poplar
And over rock, a porcupine
In the shadows, lupine willing
Daybreak. My soul remains
Spoken for by the waves,
By the night river rising.

In Praise of Black Crappies

In the descending evening darkness
the float slowly dragged into
a deeper night. The ice circle a ring
of remarkable clarity. I do
not sing, but I wish I could do so.
Instead I lift the rod and reel
in line. That thin margin stretched
between worlds: yours and mine.

The weight, the delicate power
of your fins as you pass beneath
the hole, becomes my power. I
speak gently to you to ease the long
journey you must make to the unfriendly
air. I'm huddled in dim light
and wish you upward with thanks
for your gentle passing.
Your flesh becomes my flesh.
A monument to the intrusion
of darkness, one life blending
with certainty into another.

Walking Back to the Car: Kickapoo River

Last week the stream gave up rising
and flows orderly between its banks
like words flow between margins on a page.
From downstream; voices arguing perhaps —
or perhaps in love — drift up river. I slowly
edge along the border of poplar and pasture.
I would whistle if I were not so tired, and if
a tune were not such trouble. I would sing a bit,
an old song, but I have no desire to draw
attention to myself. Instead, a woodcock
accidentally flushed, spirals toward heaven
in the dusk, all sharp and angular in flight
like the shape of desire. In that moment
I understand the timeless nature of air
and water; the timeless whispering of light.

Let's Believe

Let's believe we are spring's
First hummingbird — iridescent
At the mouth of a morning
glory. Hovering still
From blossom to blossom
Like an old man searching for
Treasure. Indecisive, determined,
Mixing sweet nectar with wing beats
And ruin. The sunlight has lead
Us north in a mysterious alchemy
Of magnetism and moonlight.
We must touch each flower
Blooming here. We must kiss
Each fragrant blossom as it
Shudders under weightless wings.

Fereydoun Faryad in Northfield

There is no thunder, no lightening,
Only a May breeze from the northwest
That remembers the winter just passed.

Water stands in low spots gathered
By infinite gravity into reflecting
Pools blue on blue on blue.

On the back road, we pass a spot
Where my son swears he saw a bear
Once, a small one, but now only crows

Gather, like poets, examining the remains
Of small creatures. No podium, just
And finally, you Fereydoun Faryad far

From home, chilly, calm, pulling the sun
Toward the horizon with quiet words. Poems
Like little bits of glass busy with reflection.

On My Decision to Stop Writing Poetry

The wind from the southwest blows
Hard, hot air over delicate topsoil until
The air holds ground like a subtle fog.
Air and dirt haze low places
The wind cannot reach.

And I join dust there clipped
By autumn's first falling leaves
And corn sleeves ripped from stalks
In the natural bowl used as a football
Stadium. A John Deere mower

Moves back and forth over a single word:
Spartans. I have decided never to write again.
I've arrived at this decision in Fergus Falls,
Minnesota, in my fifth decade just
When things should be getting good.

Greed has defeated reason in this world
And taken beauty down with it. And even
The September sunshine, and the miles
Rushing under the wheels of my car
And Bartok can't change anything

Or any one thing. And the Cooper's hawk
Circling and banking stalks defeat
In the bull rushes, and I am finished here
And broken and neither love nor eternity
Can save me now. I've turned, at the end

Of this line, my back, on these failed words forever.

Imagine It

Imagine it a stream
that flows from the north
somewhere, another state perhaps,
and it appears beneath the county
bridge suddenly, like a phone
call late at night, from someone
you once loved. Years ago,
when those things mattered.
It flows still winding slowly
and intimately among the cows
and the barbed wire and the switch grass.
Imagine its fish are friendly,
hugging the bottom in riffles
and runs, rising excitedly for hatches
as predictable as sunset.
Now imagine it all means something
with gravity as baseline data
and love waiting at the end of facts.
Search out the meaning
of words, and geology, and life's
persistent truths as persistent
as the steady tug of a trout resisting
the inevitable coming to hand.

Misrepresented as Meaning: November

Cattail seeds skiff over the surface
ice. Twenty-four degrees last night
and today snow mixes with sunshine.
Below the ice a muskrat glides
to its tunnel near shore trailed by air
bubbles that linger under the surface,
trapped. Jet contrails crisscross the sky toward
North Dakota. Building like these lines
build left to right down the page of the sky. The vapor
trail expands only to dissipate like a cloud
into a clear blue that one only imagines.
Subsonic signals the season is going
on without regard to me. Without
regard to anything except the command
of the sun; a persistent presence I record
here, misrepresented as meaning something.

South Dakota

The moonlight on wheat stubble —
jack rabbits along the fence line.
In the distance the yard's
prison of light illuminates barn doors
back step, shrubs.
A headlight questions the darkness
aimlessly headed toward town.
"Describe the night," I say to you
on the phone, and your silence
is the best description there is. I'm
not listening that well anyway
thinking instead of the great
distance that stretches between us.
What we once were and what we
have become. I mention my grief
to the indifferent stars,
wishing for the sound of a bell,
on a good hound dog,
growing louder with its
steady return.

First Snow

First snow today before noon
The taste of it on the wind
Since late last night.

Wind enters the bones
And settles in like an old friend
Who is happy to sleep on the couch

Counting these winters has become
Almost impossible lately. They blend
Into the language of the seasons creating

A grammar of their own. Building
Meaning from the ground up
First grass disappears then the lowest

Branches a reversal symbolic
Of burrowing into the darkness
Deep into the earth

Wild plums still cling to branches
Fermenting in their own skin
The tree leans against the window

Knocking to get in. But the door
Here is locked, and the key hidden
Like stars are hidden by the day-bright sky.

Hailstones

Until finally, by their own weight
Hailstones fall. They bounce
Turning in air, bounce earthward
Distant as another planet.

I plant them in the garden
Out back. By fall they've grown
Into monuments of stone
Small kisses on a distant land

After the Town Hall Forum

Hunger is the language
The poor speak. Learn
The vocabulary of that
Language. The sentence
One can make of longing
For one more grain of rice.
Dark shadows deep
Inside being – like the weeping
Of a small child that only
Knows emptiness.

A Fragile Shelter

(New Poems: 2017 – 2019)

A Hundred Fires

It is in the shelter of each other that we live
    – Irish Proverb

This is a fragile shelter
made as it is of thin bones
and promises. But the sky
is also fragile, also frail,
and it manages to support
the stars.
          And is there a choice
about living? We live because
we must. And
we live with one another,
so why not offer roof
and walls to those so much
like us. Why not huddle
in hope on this tiny island
filled with the glow of a hundred
fires. "Shelter me here," I say,
"and I will shelter you,"
the only promise that matters.

Rounding Out

The stars work heedless
They did not invent the night.
– Thomas McGrath

But the stars struck fire
the instant
the night was made.
The imagined shapes
a backdrop to narrative.
They were the paint the eye,
gazing up, employed
to create wonder.
Wonder at the persistent dark,
wonder at the dark
inside too. Looking up to imagine
dark endlessly.

Well before hand print
and blown pigment on a wall;
there were stars.

The hand print said "We are here."
And the constellations say "We imagine."
Tracing a world
across the sky, rounding out
the seasons
and all we are.

On Your Fence Surviving a Late May Storm

The wooden fence built straight, posts unmoved
by spring's frost, and solid as the promise summer
stands on. Your strength then, a young boy, proved
to move with grace to young man. Hammer
and level and twine set tight to align
the earth and stars ; align the song a heart
sings against the dark. More than a fence lies
at the heart of digging and nailing; the start,
a course of rough-hewn planks you must believe
in. Rough but getting brighter all the time
nail heads polished by hammer blows twelve
for each row. You've grown past young man now, I'm
pointing out, your road has stretched prairie wide
beyond that backyard fence the storm decides.

End of Summer Love Poem

Down the street
the raccoons
preview darkness.
They adjust
their expectations
in the face
of winter.
        We do the same
with old sheets,
against the frost,
creating another night
for tomatoes to grow.
The dog
barks at them as if they
were real intruders.
But nothing intrudes,
not thoughts,
not reflection,
not sunset.
The brussel sprouts
make slow progress
and the peppers:
orange, and red;
yellow and green,
will dry on a string
in the kitchen;
then warm us like love
all winter.
What do we really need,
my dear,
but this small room,
each other,
and the quiet mystery
at the heart

of each day.
"Nothing more." I say
out loud to no one,
and mean it.

Ashes

Ashes don't return to wood.
    – Han Shan

But the snapping turtle
buried in mud
all through the long winter
greets spring still
a snapping turtle.
Fieldstone remains fieldstone
even if
piled for a hundred years.
And the cottontail runs
in a great circle
through sumac, blow downs
and abandoned burrows
full of darkness – the voice
of ruin.
Starlight outruns
the star. We are
transformed into the sound
of emptiness. The whisper
of a breeze
beneath a crow's wing
repeats our name
and we live
like embers become ashes
after flame.

What the Carp Taught Me

At dragon's gate one must
persevere beyond the boundaries
that are set in place by men;
like these word move forward
against all odds, by building one on
the other, creating a world.
And old carp hug deep water
or snuffle in the shallows for food.
The moon sees them – through the long
day they remain – they are a gift
the world gives freely.
Understand them and we understand
earth and stars. We balance here
on rocks together
we mouth the words we love:
long vowels and golden scales,
cottonwood seeds and tiny nymphs,
always changing and always the same

like one can say of rivers.
What luck we share a world!
And share the thin line
that joins us to the other place
years away and more permanent.
Meet me there old carp
and I will thank you in a language
we both understand; a language
we learned to speak fluently
together.

The Public Hearing

They talked about the river
like it was an abandoned building
like it smelled of compound interest.

The same water where my son caught
a one eyed northern pike,
his personal dragon, released to create

horror below the railroad trestle.
I listened to people talk on,
the sun setting over riffles just upstream

the moon shone in light and shadow
the heron and the kingfisher slept,
the uncomfortable sleep of a long night,

but the bats scooped midges from the water's
surface, like the thought that all this
matters. The end before the beginning

the river singing in dark depths
as if it knew it would lose again.

November Snow

Black Capped Chickadees blink,
Back and forth; cedar to feeder.

Whitman Asleep

The apple blossoms in fog:
A rabbit chews clover
Over by the garage. Walt Whitman
How did you sleep so well?
Seeing the boys in blue fractured
By the fire of hoof beats
Threatening us all with oblivion.
Supermarket aisles with ladies
In the tomatoes. Not to mention light
Beams as meteors swing close
To earth. The catfish, Walt,
Wait in deep currents for starlight —
Those currents pulled by moonbeams.
What is not magic in this world?
What is there not to love?
Remember me, Walt, when our elements
Meet in space the stuff of stars
You there first waiting in the green
Light for me your tardy student
To finally arrive.

Poem for a Girl Reading the Odyssey at a Rest Area on Interstate 90 Near Fairmont, Minnesota

What island are you washed up on
to tell your story, after feasting;
treated as a guest should be treated
by all your gentle hosts?

Your dog, patient beneath the picnic
table until the end of your travels;
when he will love you still — rising
at your scent — his tail

sweeping air. The journey's riddles
evaporate and time still ahead.
Will the meddling gods track
your troubles? What mooring will

anchor you at home? Here Freigthtliners
pass as waves rush to shore.
Relentless as the desire to belong
somewhere. Boundless sunset just beginning,

my heart twinges at the sight:
you reading there with all your might.

A Bear

A bear awakens deep in cedar
And drags the scent of winter
With him across the swamp.
A hunger like humility stirs
In the depths of his chest.
Parts of winter remain
Like a line of fence posts
Near the edge of a wood.

A contrail crosses the sky.
It forms a highway birds could travel
But instead they flutter
And chirp, and the crows set about
Their warning.

A badger speaks the language
Of darkness still
In his burrow. His chest rises
And falls like crests on an inland
Sea. His fur flutters and his
haunches flex. It will be days
Before he stirs, up and out
Of darkness
An emissary between two worlds
And when he does rise the past
Remains burrowed deep beneath
The earth.

I walk the trails and wonder
If the great night will settle on us
All equally or if the darkness
Is only intended for me.

Will I know its dark coming
Down and reach out when it
Gets closer, reach out
To embrace nothing?

After Illness

Owl wings in the high willow
sound their whisper over
the forest floor. The long
orbit of rings growing
inside the bark of trees
like hard times in the middle
of the country.
                    Why not weigh
the hours until dark like a butcher
weighs the feast we will
sit down to. This world
will never love us back
unless love is measured
in thunderclouds and snow
drifts or lake ice cracking
like a rifle shot.
A heart rattles and shakes
in the prison of the chest,
servant not master.
Welcoming the chance to do right
heart ache better than heart break
morning better than night.

Plum Orchard
For John Koch

The plum blossoms signal morning
A semaphore of this covenant that begins
Each day like the recitation of those
Things in which we believe.
Each fragrant blossom becomes
A fragrant breeze; a litany,
Each branch a sign of hope,
And roots hug this earth shadowing
The direction of lightning.
Rings under bark like heartbeats
Wishing for rain. Meadowlark in the distance
The sound of traffic out on the boulevard.
One lone bee circles itself
Searching for a place to alight.
Finally.

The Creel

Another emptiness that needs to be filled.
So down into that darkness
I place ferns, they rest like
The voice of Adam after naming
The animals.
Through the wicker some light
Shines, and the last breath
Of daylight fills it too.
As the stars rise, they appear
Like trout their speckles
On a blue backdrop. Small brook
Trout from unnamed waters
Down along the border somewhere.
I fill the darkness with a tiny fire
And cook them slowly. In a circle
Of light.
They become me, and I gently
Place the creel back in its place
Waiting for another day
Another path to the same
Conclusion, sleep, heartbeats,
The song of creatures making their way
In the darkness that stretches
To morning.

Williston, North Dakota

It didn't begin like this;
it once contained only grass
and wind along the horizon,
and out here it is *all* horizon,
occasionally an oil pump would move
like a prehistoric beast sucking
oil. But after the thumping trucks
pounded earth to jiggle subterranean
substrate, GPS coordinates like buoys
on an inland sea, marked
this spot forever.
                      Souls and their stories
poured in. The poor at gas pumps
with hope just behind their eyes.
They slept anywhere like seeds
lying dormant; big bluestem
side oats, Indian grass: waiting.
Man camps spread outward —
families left back in Iowa or Oklahoma
or Missouri.
                The only thing that doesn't
grow is the post office " No one here
writes letters," Eunice at the window
says. And workers lose a little
of their story each day. Words fail.
On each pump, the polishing rod
and the sucking rod drains oil
heavenward. Drains the soul
so Minneapolis and Chicago
can waste at their present rate.
The prairie watches;
sends rain storms and lightning.

It is it.

The prairie, patient as forever.
saw the triceratops disappear
saw the Dakota expand with the buffalo
saw Russian settlers bake black bread
and dream of home, like we dream
of home far from this. Our own story
owned by us again. The story
each worker tells to the night sky.

Buffalo Gap National Grasslands
For Antelope

Snowed on all night, this land
breathes moisture, the first in months,
into gray clay and lichens. Holding it in
a minute before exhaling a light breeze.
It smells of sage, and time.
So severe it reminds me of the night sky.
An expanse stretched to the border
of what time creates out there: space.
Constantly expanding, constantly
making more, an abundance of nothing,
if grass *is* nothing,
out to the horizon. And these gullies,
like creases on an old man's hand,
complex as the constant geography
of back road — country gravel — that still
can't encompass all this emptiness.

Antelope, like an afterthought, appear
along the horizon or down a fence line
out of nowhere, like new planets
discovered by accident. And we two hunters
crawl into the wind, crawl over
the crown of the hill, to find them
disappeared, like certainty.
And we lie there for a minute, our bellies
to the earth, amazed at the miracle
just vanished. The magic of Antelope.
A trick we accept; like hope, or cold
or the astonishment at the horizon still
miles distant.

Addressing the Stones

If you must address the stones
speak as if talking
to a wise grandfather.
The stone will know if you mean
it, and rise up out of the dark
and follow your voice.

When you speak to the stones,
there's no need for melody or melancholy
the stones shape words their own way.
A covenant with stones looks
like chicken bones and badger burrows.

The stones, free from ground,
feel light, feel weightless. Far
enough away from earth, stones
could paint the sky with fire
erasing time, stretching out forever.
But most importantly, when talking

to the stones use the language of children.
Build a wall with it, a wall made entirely
of stone, to keep the world in
and everything else out.

Gideon's Marsh: November

Morning quickens within the boundaries
of light. The big ducks come down on
a winter wind out of Canada: canvas backs,
blue bills, red heads. They shudder, cup their
wings, and prepare to sit down
in the empty space at the cattail's heart.
Water's invitation is all openness,
swells and waves suggest decisions
along the edges of the marsh.
Muck and distilled thoughts in wet
coldness; iron-like, flat, gray reflection.
Consider the confines of wind and water
the gestures engendered by the failure
of dreams, and how a world is disassembled
by beating wings, by breath, by
the division of days into hours.

To It All

Each morning, in the dark,
the years number my bones.
Knees are cranes that slowly wake.
The right shoulder a snail unfurling
and these hands stiff from carrying
heavy burdens. But like words
everything awakens. This body
a cottage of feathers borrowed
from the brightest birds.
The doorway like a mouth calling
out the names of animals
badger, red pole, hawk. Naming
the world this body loves
more than it has loved anything,
it keeps playing its song through
quiet and cinders, asphalt and air.
The dragonfly and carp, trout
and hare, call me to action
to all of it: to it all.

At Dusk

Bats at dusk
Sweep midges
From the water's surface.
They dodge like a song
Shared between equals.
The water flows
As counterpoint
And wheels circle
Within circles
All up and down
The bank.
Sunset dims
Hushed thoughts
Of day. Be here:
With water and
Small brown bats,
Defining air.

At the Saw

Chainsaw, oil, gas, redemption,
this tree, our view for fifteen years
the place of Cooper's hawk, brown bat,
gray squirrel and framing white tailed deer
raccoon and coyote.
                      Split finally
by freeze and thaw, thunderstorm
and dark spirits. South of our bedroom,
and if it fell, by my gloomy geometry,
its top branches would tickle
the kitchen window,
                          or given inaccuracy
in my estimate, a likely case, crash
through the wall and into the kitchen
sink.
        So today I calculate its line of fall
the angle the chainsaw handle must
create. I clear my route at forty-five
degrees for quick escape
for safety's sake, and my withdrawal.
Wedge and maul secure I pause
entertaining the politics of blue sky
I'll be creating and sunlight
like a small god working toward
a day of rest, creation but in reverse.
Hope at first that seeds regret.

The Hog

Old friend, there is no way
to save you. No way to save
me either. Let us eat
the corn-cob and all. And wallow
afterward in mud up to our ears;
a noble grave of soil and sunlight.
Why not? And we can wish,
wish for a sharp blade and sudden
darkness. The light once
out remains so. Our
heaven, old friend, is behind us.
All stars blink out at dawn.

A Next Night

These small paths through undergrowth and ruin
barely discernible in leaf litter and ferns,
the route our thoughts take as we
descend into what is left of the wild.
A half-acre is a wilderness world
and scale is like a dream that only
means something when we awaken
or tell it to a friend. The smell of earth
and decay, a perfume like no other
contains hints of our better self, when
each breath still held the scent of reptiles.
That self that walks the house
at 2:00 A.M. wondering about the self.
Going out to others in the summer heat.
A bridge, a river shrunken by dry weather.
Dragonflies, pull us inexorably forward
into a new day, into a next night.

Moored

Moored. The solid weight
Of pilings, wood like an anchor,
And the flood of sunlight following a path
Across the sky. The elements conspire
Here in silence. Winter sounds forming
A promise that lasts for months
And that holds in its being — change,
Regular as a heartbeat.
"Wait here," it seems to say,
And feel the season dematerialize
Listen to the tune the winter wind
Sings. It contains the notes
Of spring.

Monarch
For Bob White

Return to water
to shoreline
the thinnest path
the finest border.

The kingdom of sky
and shadow
the sun uneasy
on the temples of light.

Bone and rock
mute commands
that signal worlds
are turning.

A mind changing.
Trust gravity flowing
to the sea.

Its voice a color
the tone of water
flowing down

and widening out.

Mending

Like those parts of me
That must be made whole
Those parts I don't recall
Being broken, but instead are like clouds
Descending
A soul tugged beneath the surface.
I must recover, repair,
Set things right, atone.
Current seams make their own rules
I can't see.
The water reflecting just tells me
About me. I'm doubled, and therefore
Mend to make things right,
The drift true. All set back in motion
Like a hundred sparrows
Gathered in a stream-side pine
Their tiny bones whisper
"Live without weight in this world."

Balance
Based on a mistranslation from the Spanish

I grief you my window.
Hope flutters farther
down the street
engendering solitude.

I ruin you my window.
The light that becomes
us most, unfolding flower
source of fire.

I assume you my window.
A door, a floor, a view
where balance lives
only half the time.

After Death

The night sky above Minneapolis
inhabited by constellations and nothing.
I am nothing too, but
remain the stuff of stars.

Thinking back I recall only trees,
and a perfect brook
humming ahead,
signaling my return.
My homecoming.
The chain is gone,
the margin disappeared.

A Picture Frame

In the back of the car
there's a picture frame
left from yesterday's trip
to the thrift store donation
bin. I hold it up and it
contains switchgrass and big
bluestem. The edges hug the frame
like tractors hug
the roadside ditch. When I place
it on the ground by the front
tire, mullein and side oats
swirl from stalk, to stem,
to syllables, guttering between
margins on a page,
order in four squared
corners. Order in lines on a road,
marking the limits of what
we see, framing ideas
and fathering the map.
These deer inhabit it.
These beetles and bees transects
its heart. These fish rise too
instinctively. A clear drinking
glass left on a log where wood
was split. One lone Kestrel
slips like a brainstorm in and out
of the frame from above.
The sound of frail voices
echoing downstream.

Mallard Island: A Triptych

1

Dragonflies test the air
and decide misquotes
can figure it out on their
own — no need to interfere
until autumn signals sumac
to turn to winter
as dew gives up hope
to frost slowly sorting it all out.
All of it.
The breeze, the early sunset,
the flowers expiring as if
this were all planned
as if air needed to be
reminded it is air.

2

Deer mouse can't find
a beginning, middle, or end,
neither can the darkness,
so how can either know their
place in the story?
The melody of sunlight
through pines dematerializes
in fragrance and light
outward from some center
like time. The deer mouse
knows this, then this over here
divided yet singular like now.
A link in some chain
drawn tight.

3

There is a pillar of sunlight
dusted in pollen reflected
and blinking like shards of glass
in some parking lot. You hop
just then from the edge of juniper
and I'm forced by your form
to consider ears; the monarchy
of sound.
Your flank ripples in dew,
and your gaze the gaze
of all prey, that never
has the comfort of knowing
peace, and instead just knows alert
and more alert. My harmlessness
means nothing to you neither
does my love. Just as suddenly
you have disappeared, despite
my watching, a magician's trick
varying the old theme. The invisible
made visible, slight of hand
right before my eyes.

Pastoral

In the high pasture,
at dawn, the lamb just born
refused its mother's milk,
a death warrant to be replaced
with death itself if
something wasn't done,
and on the radio the shepherd
instructed me to tickle the lamb
behind the knee, and sure
the lamb began to feed.
Ewe's milk rich as a sunny meadow
a lesson in wonder
of a waning day and the progress
of life and its resistance.
When you, a boy child, was born
and resisted as did the little ram
your mother's milk and she, astonished
as any meadow flower, wept
at what to do, the lamb came
then to mind. Strong, still, like you became,
and I showed her: tickle here behind
the left knee, and you in your
own time drank deeply.
What a secret that.
The shepherd's view, the long
step, the light touch, and home.

Cambrian Blackbirds

Blackbirds flock, like night, in trees,
they sound a warning that sinks
as if into a dark burrow.
If I take away dirt
I get a larger emptiness.
If I remove blackbirds
I get silence; each dusk
a question of time.
Blackbirds circle each morning
before going off to feed and I
am left with the balance of a day
to build on. Today, I search
the Cambrian layer for shells
remnants of coral branching
like a tree; loaded down
with dark angels and starlight,
birds and rock,
thistles and dew.

Daley Creek

He swears he hears a voice,
talking, not to him
but in the background.
A radio in a car perhaps parked
up on the road?
But no. The sound of something
saying words. Is it the rocks
or watercress whispering the
secret of sunlight?
Or some spirit addressing
the fear of one alone.
Belief in uncertainty.
The air thick
with electricity and the wingbeats
of tiny insects
reminding air it is still air.

School Begins

The birds line phone wires
along county seven,
and between the rows
of soybeans, caterpillars
wander like shoppers
searching for a bargain
on a winter coat.
The fox burrow up
on a hill near the tree line
has bones scattered
at its entrance. Bones
of small, unnamed creatures now
turned magically into fox, fueling his
run along the edge between
trees and crops — the border
of things, much as summer borders
autumn. Transient messages
about change,
about moving on. A lesson
planned in advance
by the rotating earth
and by the declining sunlight
and by our wishes
for tomorrow, or the next day,
or with luck, the day after that.

Wardrobe

I would make my clothes of wild things
of crabapple and buckthorn
of honeysuckle and bittersweet.
A vest of dew and shoes of gneiss
a billion years old. Flecked with mica
and fools gold.
My hat a full moon echoing
rising oceans, summoning
the tides, and I would love
you like a northwest breeze
building to the cool silence of a
thunderstorm. And the gentle
falling of the stars all night.
Until in the morning I
wonder if it was just a dream,
or if I imagined it all like a really good story.
Either one, so much better than real life.
Better than earth, better than sky or flesh.

Christmas Morning South of Faribault, MN

A blue spruce out of place here
with bittersweet
twined on its south side the vine's
orange fruit; autumn's promise,
still hanging like one final
question against blue sky,
on the north side's branches:
snow. Light, a dusting
they call it. Dusting.
Two cardinals decorate
the uppermost branches
scarlet hosts searching
for food.
In the distance, three bells
one on the collar of each beagle
busy sifting scent in wild raspberry
sumac and Russian olive,
and above the bells, the sound
of voices mother, son, laughing
in knee deep snow.
Which of these gifts do I deserve?
None of them, I think,
then I reconsider and realize
I deserve them all. Unasked for
and echoing down through
the years, years full
of gratitude and heartbeats
as one hound's plaintive voice
rises above all of it
then two more. Simple as
the wishes we all hold dear.

Deer at Six A.M.

Two deer graze along the edge
of a wood. The sun just rising
casts its wonder of light
and shadow. They blaze up
almost orange and touched
with dew.
We walk the field, wet
ourselves, to the knee.
We don't talk but instead we
forgive the edge of all things
where worlds join. What
will take us farther?
What secret is in each heart?
What flame burns in us
for tomorrow or the next day?
The deer turn slowly, unafraid,
and disappear silently into
sumac and buckthorn.
We continue on up the hill
and around a bend, glimpsing
the eye, the forked antlers,
the metaphor of two sets
of perfect tracks, fresh
as a new wound.

Half the Table

On a morning when the world is empty
nothing to put on paper
except another nod to nothing.
A morning when the cardinals
fail to gather on the feeder
for some reason
their flash and flight
usually a scarlet excuse
to use the word scarlet.
A morning when cars
don't even pass. Their exhaust
I could compare to breath if I was lazy.
And of even more concern,
inside I feel exactly nothing.
Not passion, not desire, not rage
or hunger. And the dog
doesn't sit curled at my feet.
Sensing like only dogs in poems can,
what moves me.
There is nothing today.
No mystery no glimpse of the eternal,
however permanent
no morning song,
to reaffirm
the passing of hours alone
as sun rises,
and of course,
no poem at the end of all this sitting.
Nothing. Suddenly, I realize
as someone probably already said.
There is only writing
and getting ready to write.
All the rest is waiting.
The sun wonders through the window,
settling on exactly half the table.

No Leaving

In this world there is no leaving
we exist wherever we've been
binary, static, indelible. And flesh
we all know is a temporary diversion.
Eroding like a river bank, like striations
on a prairie hillside facing west. Erosion,
that reveals fossils from another time.
Aligning our soul with our life somehow.
Storm clouds build over South Dakota,
and the finches tweet and twitter
their response. I do what I have always
done and consider it all a success.

This practice as a kind of perfection
the practice of a practice, becomes prayer.
The sea swells with each full moon.
Each story a little glimpse at eternity.

Driving from Willow to Bee Creek

Cows amble down the middle
of the road in front of me,
pasture to pasture.
I drive from one stream
to another, slowly, trying not
to kick up dust, trying not
to rush these great
beasts. They deserve time. Their
mighty flanks shift back and forth;
the radio warns of bombing runs
cancelled in Iran. In Spain, a cork shortage.
I wish the news could
not reach me today, but like the endless chain
of thoughts, always in my head,
I can't turn the radio
off. I take comfort:
in moving water, in speckled sunlight,
in the quiet lowing of cows;
the dry flies in my chest pocket,
and in all those impulses in the world I
will never understand.

Brick Tender

All summer the scaffolding
reached to heaven, and I looked
up my neck aching and knowing
those heights were not mine.
I worked in mud, mortar, brick.
The stuff of this earth,
but I obeyed commands
from above. Stiffer
or looser in the mix, more
or less until it is just right,
but it is never just right.
So the day is divided into
caught up, and just a bit behind.

"He's a good hand," I overhear
the mason say,
in an accent
from somewhere else,
and I take those words
home with me that night along
with my black lunch box,
and a quart of cold beer,
and years later,
I build with them
this poem.

About the Author

Larry Gavin is the author of these books: *Necessities, Least Resistance, Stone and Sky, The Initiation of Praise,* and *A Fragile Shelter: New and Selected Poems.* In addition to poetry, he was senior editor at *Midwest Fly Fishing Magazine* for fifteen years and currently writes for *Minnesota Outdoor News.*

He lives in Faribault, Minnesota, spends much of his time fly fishing for smallmouth bass and trout, and wandering the woods with his small pack of beagles all fall and winter.

www.ingramcontent.com/pod-product-compliance
Lightning Source LLC
Chambersburg PA
CBHW030937090426
42737CB00007B/455